Is f

D0246399

RUSHING RIVERS

Collector Card

RUSHING RIVERS

Collector Card

RUSHING RIVERS

Collector Card

RUSHING RIVERS

Collector Card

Nile river

The river of the ancient pharaohs
and the world's longest river.

SCORE

LENGTH: 6695 km — 10
NUMBER OF COUNTRIES: eleven — 10
PEOPLE LIVING NEAR: 175 million — 5
DISCHARGE: 5100 m³ per second — 2

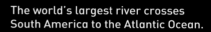

Amazon river

The world's largest river crosses
South America to the Atlantic Ocean.

SCORE

LENGTH: 6437 km — 9
NUMBER OF COUNTRIES: seven — 7
PEOPLE LIVING NEAR: 20 million — 1
DISCHARGE: 219,000 m³ per second — 10

Yangtze river

The longest river in Asia flows
through beautiful gorges.

SCORE

LENGTH: 6300 km — 8
NUMBER OF COUNTRIES: one — 1
PEOPLE LIVING NEAR: 430 million — 10
DISCHARGE: 31,900 m³ per second — 6

Yellow river (Huang He)

The Yellow river floods so often that
it is called the 'River of Sorrows'.

SCORE

LENGTH: 5464 km — 7
NUMBER OF COUNTRIES: one — 1
PEOPLE LIVING NEAR: 175 million — 5
DISCHARGE: 2110 m³ per second — 1

It's all about…

RUSHING RIVERS

KINGFISHER

KINGFISHER

First published 2015 by Kingfisher
an imprint of Pan Macmillan
a division of Macmillan Publishers International Ltd
20 New Wharf Road, London N1 9RR
Associated companies throughout the world
www.panmacmillan.com

Series editor: Sarah Snashall
Series design: Little Red Ant
Adapted from an original text by Claire Llewellyn and Thea Feldman

ISBN 978-0-7534-3893-0

Copyright © Macmillan Children's Books 2015

9 8 7 6 5 4 3 2 1

1TR/0415/WKT/UG/128MA

A CIP catalogue record for this book is available from the British Library.

Printed in China

Picture credits
The Publisher would like to thank the following for permission to reproduce their material.
Top = t; Bottom = b; Centre = c; Left = l; Right = r
Cover Shutterstock/Dziewul; Back cover Shutterstock/Evgeni Stefanov; Pages 2–3, 30–31
Shutterstock/Johnny Lye; 4 Shutterstock/Teri Virbickis; 5t Shutterstock/Evgeni Stefanov;
5b Shutterstock/bumhills; 6–7 Kingfisher Artbank; 7 Shutterstock/V.Borisov; 8 Shutterstock/
Light & Magic Photography; 9t Shutterstock/Przemyslaw Skibinksi; 9b Shutterstock/
B.S.Karan; 10 Shutterstock/szefei; 10b Shutterstock/Kang Khoon Seang; 11 Shutterstock/
Jody; 12–13, 13b Shutterstock/Christian Vinces; 13t Shutterstock/Anton_Ivanov;
14 Shutterstock/Evgeny Dubinchuk; 15 Shutterstock/RM Nunes; 16–17 Shutterstock/Anton_
Ivanov; 16b, 17t Shutterstock/guentermanaus; 18 Shutterstock/Pongthorn S; 19 Shutterstock/
Elena Elisseeva; 19t Shutterstock/Bazru; 20 Shutterstock/Sihasakprachum; 21 Shutterstock/
panda3800; 22–23 Shutterstock/Andy Z; 23 Corbis/Otto Lang; 24–25 Shutterstock/Dan
Breckwoldt; 25t Getty/Travel Ink; 25b Kingfisher Artbank, 26 Shutterstock/Rock and Wasp;
27 Shutterstock/Matt Jepson; 27b Shutterstock/mypokcik; 28–29 Shutterstock/Dragana
Gerasimoski; 29 Flickr/NCVO London; 32 Shutterstock/aabeele
Cards: Front tl Shutterstock/WitR; tr Shutterstock/Ajancso; bl Shutterstock/jejim; br Getty/
Keren Su; Back tl Shutterstock/American Spirit; tr Shutterstock/Stephanie Periquet;
bl Shutterstock/darkpurplebear; br Shutterstock/szefei

CONTENTS

Rushing rivers

Rivers can be gushing torrents or narrow streams. A river can be wide, narrow, fast or slow along its route or at different times of the year.

FACT...

It is hard to see the other side of the Mississippi river at its widest point. It is 17 kilometres across!

Rivers are home to lots of animals and plants, and many people live along their banks.

Kingfishers build their nests in river banks and feed on freshwater fish.

SPOTLIGHT: Nile river

Record breaker:	longest river in the world
Length:	6695 km
Location:	travels through 11 countries
Animals:	crocodiles, hippos, fish

From mountain to sea

The beginning of a river is
called its source. From there,
the river flows downhill
towards the sea.

The river flows
fast downhill.

The river gets bigger as other
rivers and streams join it.

The river reaches flatter ground
and slows down. It snakes across
the land in big curves.

The oystercatcher finds snails and worms in the mud at the mouth of a river.

The river flows into the sea. This part is called its mouth.

7

Shaping the land

Moving water is very powerful. As a river flows across the land, it carves the riverbed and chips at the banks. On limestone hills, rainwater soaks down through the rock. The water drains into underground rivers that erode, or wear away, tunnels and caves.

This cave has been carved out by an underground river.

Sometimes a river flows over a cliff that it cannot wear away. This creates a waterfall.

The mist from Victoria Falls in southern Africa can be seen 20 kilometres away.

SPOTLIGHT: Victoria Falls

Record breaker:	largest waterfall in the world
Height:	108 m
Location:	Zambezi river
Fact:	twice height of Niagara Falls

FACT...

The Grand Canyon, USA, was carved out by the Colorado river over 3 million years ago.

9

River plants

Rivers make good habitats for plants because plants need water to grow. Trees that grow alongside rivers have long roots to grip the soil. These roots help to protect the river.

Trees grow along a river in a rainforest in Malaysia.

Giant water lilies have roots underwater.

Plants are important to the life of the river. Their leaves give off a gas called oxygen, which fish and other river life need to breathe. Plants also provide food for animals and safe places to nest or hide.

Reeds make perfect nesting places for water birds.

River animals

Rivers are home to many kinds of fish, frogs and newts. In hot countries reptiles such as turtles, crocodiles and snakes live in rivers.

Most rivers worldwide are home to snails, shrimps, beetles and worms. Many insects, such as dragonflies, live in the water for the first stage of their life.

river turtles

Crocodiles live in rivers in Africa and North and South America.

Water voles nest in holes in river banks. Water birds look for plants to eat, while otters and kingfishers hunt for fish.

A giant otter hunts for fish.

Rivers and people

Many of the world's oldest and most important cities were built on river banks: Cairo is on the River Nile, Rome is on the Tiber and London is on the River Thames.

New York was built at the mouth of the Hudson river.

Thousands of people bathe in the River Ganges in India each year. It is worshipped as a goddess in the Hindu religion.

Some rivers have a special meaning for people. The Ganges river in India is sacred to Hindus; the River Jordan is sacred to Jews, Muslims and Christians.

SPOTLIGHT: Ganges river

Record breaker: most sacred river to Hindus
Length: 2525 km
Location: India and Bangladesh
Animals: Ganges river dolphins, gharials

15

The mighty Amazon

The Nile is the longest river in the world, but the Amazon is the largest. In the wet season it can be 40 kilometres wide in places.

The Amazon river is home to over 3000 species of fish including the deadly piranha. Anacondas, Amazon river dolphins and turtles are also found swimming in its waters.

Piranhas have sharp teeth and can attack and kill humans.

FACT...

There is only one bridge over the Amazon river, the Manaus-Iranduba bridge in Brazil.

SPOTLIGHT: Amazon river

Record breaker:	largest river in the world
Length:	6437 km
Location:	Brazil, Colombia, Peru
Animals:	anacondas, river dolphins

Using river water

In our homes we use river water for drinking, washing and flushing the toilet. Factories use huge amounts of water to make things, and to cool down machinery. Farmers use water for their animals and to irrigate their crops.

Waterwheels use the energy from fast-running water to drive machines.

If we take too much water from rivers, it may destroy the homes of the animals that live in them. This affects other animals and people, who rely on rivers for food.

Farmers use big machines like this to irrigate their crops.

Rivers and floods

When snow suddenly melts, or heavy rain falls quickly, rivers can overflow and flood the land. Sudden floods can destroy buildings and crops, and people and animals may drown.

In parts of south-east Asia, heavy rains often cause terrible floods.

These farmers in Thailand are planting rice in flooded fields.

Some rivers flood every year and this can be useful for farmers. In many countries, rice farmers rely on rivers to flood their rice crops.

FACT...

In ancient Egypt, the River Nile flooded every year. The fertile mud helped crops to grow. Good harvests helped Egypt and its people to prosper.

Dams and water power

When a dam is built across a river, a big lake called a reservoir collects behind the dam. This reservoir stores fresh water, which is piped to people's homes.

The Hoover Dam is on the Colorado river in the USA.

When water is released through tunnels in the dam, the power of the water can be turned into electricity. A quarter of the world's electricity is made from water power.

The Abu Simbel temple was relocated when Egypt's Aswan Dam was built.

FACT...

When the Aswan Dam was built across the River Nile, about 100,000 people had to be moved.

Transport by water

The longest rivers cross countries and continents. People use them for transporting goods and for travel and adventure.

Huge barges transport goods to and from factories along the River Rhine, in Germany.

Riverboats come in many shapes and sizes. There are small ferries, pleasure boats and large cruise ships like floating hotels.

A cruise ship on the Yangtze river in China.

About 200 years ago, two explorers called Meriwether Lewis and William Clark travelled over 12,500 kilometres across America along rivers to reach the Pacific coast.

A peaceful paddle down a river.

Fun on the river

Many rivers are beautiful places where people can relax and have fun. In places where the water flows slowly, people enjoy swimming or boating. In places where the river flows swiftly, kayaking is an exciting river sport.

Many people enjoy fishing in rivers as a fun sport. If they catch a fish, they may quickly free the hook from the fish's mouth and return it to the water.

Dragon-boats race along the rivers in China. The rowers pull the oars in time with the beating drum.

Save your river!

People can easily pollute rivers. Factories pour their waste into rivers or pump warm water into them after using it to cool machines. Fertilizers from farms run into the water. All this waste can harm river life.

Adding dirty water to rivers harms plant and animal life.

FACT...

Every year in the USA, thousands of people help to clean up local rivers. So far, 900 tonnes of rubbish have been removed from the water.

Volunteers clear rubbish out of the River Wandle in London, United Kingdom.

How to help rivers
- Save water whenever you can
- Join a wildlife group
- Don't throw litter or other waste into rivers or streams

GLOSSARY

banks The sides of a river.

crops Plants grown by farmers for food.

dam A wall built across a river to hold back the water.

discharge The amount of water that flows out of a river every second.

fertile Having good soil where plants grow well.

fertilizer A chemical added to soil to make it more fertile.

fresh water Water in rivers, lakes and ice that is not salty like seawater.

habitat The place where a particular animal or plant lives.

harvest The time when crops are ripe and ready to be picked.

irrigate To water the land.

limestone A type of rock that is made up of bits of animal shells.

pollute To make poisonous or unclean by adding chemicals or rubbish.

prosper To have a good life because you have everything you need.

reservoir A lake where water is stored for use.

sacred Special or holy to people of a particular religion.

source The place where a river starts.

INDEX

RUSHING RIVERS

Collector Card

RUSHING RIVERS

Collector Card

RUSHING RIVERS

Collector Card

RUSHING RIVERS

Collector Card

Collect all the titles in this series!

BEASTLY
BUGS
FREE Collector Cards and Downloadable Audio!

DEADLY
DINOSAURS
FREE Collector Cards and Downloadable Audio!

FREEZING
POLES
FREE Collector Cards and Downloadable Audio!

RIOTOUS
RAINFORESTS
FREE Collector Cards and Downloadable Audio!

RUSHING
RIVERS
FREE Collector Cards and Downloadable Audio!

SCARY
SPIDERS
FREE Collector Cards and Downloadable Audio!

SNAPPY
SHARKS
FREE Collector Cards and Downloadable Audio!

SUPER
SOLAR SYSTEM
FREE Collector Cards and Downloadable Audio!

VIOLENT
VOLCANOES
FREE Collector Cards and Downloadable Audio!

WILD
WEATHER
FREE Collector Cards and Downloadable Audio!